Bud‹

*Buddhism For Beginners –
Buddhist Teachings For Living A
Life Of Happiness, Peace, and
Enlightenment (Buddhism
Rituals, Buddhism Teachings,
Zen Buddhism, Meditation and
Mindfulness)*

Kevin Gise © 2016

Disclaimer:

This book is for informational purposes only and the author, his agents, heirs, and assignees do not accept any responsibilities for any liabilities, actual or alleged, resulting from the use of this information.

This report is not "professional advice." The author encourages the reader to seek advice from a professional where any reasonably prudent person would do so. While every reasonable attempt has been made to verify the information contained in this eBook, the author and his affiliates cannot assume any responsibility for errors, inaccuracies or omissions, including omissions in transmission or reproduction.

Any references to people, events, organizations, or business entities are for educational and illustrative purposes only, and no intent to falsely characterize, recommend, disparage, or injure is intended or should be so construed. Any results stated or implied are consistent with general results, but this means results can and will vary. The author, his agents, and assigns, make no promises or guarantees, stated or implied. Individual results will vary and this work is supplied strictly on an "at your own risk" basis.

Introduction

First off, thank you for purchasing my book "Buddhism: Buddhism For Beginners – Buddhist Teachings For Living A Life Of Happiness, Peace, and Enlightenment (Buddhism Rituals, Buddhism Teachings, Zen Buddhism, Meditation and Mindfulness)". By purchasing this book, you've shown that you're serious about learning Buddhism and trying to become your best self.

Buddhism is practiced by close to 300 million people worldwide. It's an ancient religion that's been around for thousands of years. The term Buddhism is taken from the word "bodhi" which means "to awaken" and was brought into prominence by a man called Siddhartha Gautama, now commonly referred to as the Buddha. The Buddha became enlightened or awakened at around 35 years of age and spent the remaining 45 years of his life traveling the country, teaching his beliefs to everyone from servants to noblemen. Through the centuries his teachings have been passed down and developed into the forms of Buddhism being practiced today.

Buddhists practice daily in an effort to develop inner peace, kindness, and wisdom. They do this, not only for themselves, but so they can share there sense of enlightenment with others in order to make the world a better place.

Many believe Buddhism to be less a religion and more a way of life. It's often termed as a philosophy because it seeks out wisdom. In short, Buddhism is normally summarized as trying to lead a moral life, being aware and mindful of your actions and thoughts, while developing wisdom and understanding.

Practicing Buddhism and making it a part of your daily life will allow you to understand yourself and the world in new and exciting ways. It will empower you to overcome any tribulations or adversity that is thrown in your direction. It will help to improve your overall sense of well being, while also developing mindfulness. In short, the goal of Buddhism is to help you find eternal happiness.

This book will touch on a lot of different Buddhist topics, along with providing you some insights, resources and inspirational quotes to help you during the course of your journey. Becoming a Buddhist is not a change that happens overnight. It will take some time and work on your end. However, the amount of effort you put in is absolutely worth it in the long run.

I'm sure you're ready to begin.. Let's get started!

Chapter One: Buddhism Terminology

In this chapter, you will learn:

- Buddhism Terminology

Buddhism Terminology

When first starting out there's a lot of new terminology that gets thrown around. I decided to put this section first so you could get an idea of what some of the terminology is before I start using it throughout the book, or you see it mentioned elsewhere during further studies.

I suggest reading over this section now and then referencing it when needed. This is by no means a definitive terminology guide. This is just a small sample to help get you started in your studies.

Abandonment – This refers to a true cessation. It is an empty mind devoid of fault or delusion.

Abhidharma / Abhidhamma – This is the third section in Buddhist canon that is devoted to philosophy and human psychology.

Anapanasati – This is having mindfulness of your breathing.

Anatta – Not self or insubstantial. This is one of the 3 characteristics of our existence.

Anicca – Impermanent. Another of the 3 characteristics of our existence. Buddhism teaches us that all physical and mental phenomena aren't permanent. Nothing will stay as it is and nothing will last.

Arahant - Enlightened one. This is someone who is free of any defilement. This is someone no longer a part of our cyclical existence.

Awareness - Every mind is included in the sense and mental awareness. Included are five different kinds of sense awareness. These are ear awareness, eye awareness, body awareness, tongue awareness, and nose awareness. There are also two different kinds of mental awareness. These are non conceptual and conceptual awareness.

Beginner's Mind – This is a mind open to experiencing the moment. This is a mind that is free of any conceptual overlay.

Bhikkhu – This is a Buddhist monk.

Bhikkhuni - This is a Buddhist nun.

Blessing – This is our mind being transformed from a negative to positive state. It is our mind going from a state of unhappiness and weakness to one of happiness and strength. It does so through inspiration of the holy beings. For example Buddha, our spiritual guide, or a bodhisattva.

Bodhi – Awakening or Enlightenment.

Bodhicitta – Known as wisdom heart. This is a heart or mind that has been awakened.

Bodhisattva / Bodhisatta – Someone that has taken the vow to be a completely enlightened Buddha. This is someone with complete availability and readiness to help all living beings.

Bodhi Tree – This is the tree that the Buddha attained his enlightenment under.

Brahma-Vihara – This is a sublime or heavenly abode. The four states of mind that are said to lead to one's rebirth in the heavenly realm. These are compassion, loving kindness, equanimity, and appreciative joy.

Buddha – This is a fully awakened being. Also refers to the actual Buddha who was born over 2,500 years ago in India.

Buddha-Dharma / Buddha-Dhamma – These are the actual teachings of the original Buddha.

Confession – This is the purification of our negative karma using the four kinds of opponent powers. These are the powers of reliance, force, regret, and promise.

Consciousness – We each have six primary minds or consciousnesses. These include ear, eye, body, nose, mental, and tongue consciousness.

Dana – Generosity. This is learning the ability to give. It's the first quality that needs to be perfected for someone to become Enlightened and become a Buddha.

Delusion – This is a mental factor that comes about from attention that's not appropriate, while attempting to make our mind uncontrolled and less peaceful. There are three primary delusions. These are desire, anger, and ignorance. From these delusions all the other kinds spring forth. Those include things like pride and jealousy.

Dependent Origination – This doctrine states that all physical and mental phenomena will both arise and eventually pass away dependent on conditions and causes.

Dhammapada – The most well known of the Buddhist scriptures. In total it's 423 verses that were spoken by Buddha himself. These verses focus on mental training and ethical conduct.

Dukkha – Anything temporary. Suffering. This includes both physical and mental pain. It's the first Noble Truth . It acknowledged that suffering is a reality.

Ego – This is our pattern of habits we've conditioned in ourselves over time that we often mistake as a sense of actual self.

Enlightenment – Awakening. A feeling tone.

Investigation – Inquiry or interest into an experience. One of the factors of Enlightenment.

Jhana – Mental absorption. This is a state consisting of strong concentration which suspends, temporarily, the five hindrances,

Kalyana Mitta – This is a spiritual friend. Teachers are commonly referred to in this manor.

Karma – Action or deed. This is a law known as cause and effect. It's any intentional action either good or bad that brings either unpleasant or pleasant results.

Kilesa – Defilement. These are undesirable qualities. It is a factor of our mind that keeps us from seeing things clearly.

Karuna – Compassion.

Mental Noting – This is a technique that is used when meditating to help focus our mind on the object of our meditation.

Merit – This is a wholesome action which helps to bring about good karmic results.

Metta – Loving kindness or gentle friendship. This teaching helps to cultivate our normal capacity of a loving and open heart. This practice leads to the further development of fearlessness, concentration, love, and happiness.

Middle Way – Discovered by Buddha, this is a spiritual path that tries to avoid self indulgence and self mortification.

Mudita – Empathetic or appreciative joy. This is the development of our being happy when we see other people's happiness and good fortune.

Neutral Person – This is someone you feel no disliking or liking to.

Nirvana – This is the liberation and freedom from our cyclical existence.

Pali – An ancient language used in the Theravada Buddhism scriptures.

Panna – Wisdom. Known as one of our five spiritual faculties.

Parami – These are the qualities in our character that need perfecting in order to attain Enlightenment.

Precept – This is a principle that sets a standard for our ethical conduct. This is the foundation of each Buddhist meditation that we practice.

Piti – This is a gladdening of the body and mind. It is one of the factors necessary for Enlightenment.

Uddhacca-Kukkucca – This is a hindrance of meditation. It's an agitation of our mind.

Saddha – Confidence. Faith. This is one of our five spiritual faculties.

Samadhi – Concentration. This is a deeper state of meditation. It's one of our five spiritual faculties. It's also a factor of Enlightenment.

Samatha – This is a term that refers to the group of meditations that are aimed at practicing Samadhi.

Samsara – Rebirth. Wandering on. Known as the ocean of our worldly suffering. It's the state that's governed by our five hindrances.

Sangha – This is a community of Buddhist practitioners who have attained a direct realization on our reality.

Sankhara – Physical or mental formation.

Sati – Mindfulness. Careful attention paid to physical and mental processes. This is a key factor in meditation. This is a factor of Enlightenment.

Satipatthana – This is the four different foundations of mindfulness. These include feeling, contemplation of our body, mind, and the Buddha's own teachings on mindfulness.

Sense Doors – These are six different perceptual gates that we experience our world through.

Sila – Ethical or moral conduct. A virtue and foundation of the Buddhist practice.

Sutta or Sutra – This is a discourse from the Buddha or from a disciple of the Buddha.

Theravada – This is the path of elders. A popular form of Buddhism in many regions of Asia. Uses Vipassana meditation as a big part of its tradition.

Thina-middha - Sloth. One of the hindrances of meditation.

Three Jewels of Refuge – These are the Buddha, The Sangha and The Dharma. Practitioners of Buddhism take some refuge in the knowledge that Buddha was able to find freedom and teach the Dharma as a path towards that same freedom, while also founding the Sangha, a extremely supportive community of like minded people who follow the same path.

Tranquility – Mental and physical calm. This is a factor of Enlightenment.

Upekkha – Equanimity. This is the ability to remain impartial even during the midst of our ever changing conditions. It's a factor of Enlightenment.

Vedana – Feeling. This is the unpleasant, neutral, or pleasant feeling tone that comes with all of our experiences. It's one of the 5 aggregates.

Vicikiccha – This is the type of doubt that will undermine faith. It's a hindrance of meditation.

Vinaya – Discipline. These are the regulations and rules that govern the conduct of nuns and Buddhist monks.

Vipassana – To see things clearly. It's also referred to as insight meditation. It's being able to practice mindfulness moment to moment. This sense of careful observation and sustained awareness allows us to more fully experience pain, pleasure, fear, joy, sadness, and happiness. Over time, as our insight begins to deepen, we are able to develop peace and equanimity when faced with change. This allows us to become increasingly guided by compassion and wisdom, as we move forward in life.

Viriya – The mental and physical energy needed for us to diligently practice mindfulness. The courageous heart of our energy. It's one of the factors of Enlightenment and it's also one of the 5 spiritual faculties.

Wrong View – Our mind's proclivity towards clinging to different concepts, even at reality's expense. Thinking something selfless when it's self. Thinking something is permanent that is impermanent.

Yogi – Someone undertaking a spiritual path towards awakening.

Chapter Two: An Introduction to Buddhism

In this chapter, you will learn:

- A Brief History of The Buddha
- Difference Between Buddhism & Other Types of Religion
- Forms of Buddhism
- Buddhist Concepts

A Brief History of The Buddha

So before we dive into Buddhism, let's first start with the Buddha. Born as a tribal prince in Nepal around 566 BC, Siddhartha Gautama lived in comfort during much of his early years. He was shielded from all knowledge of suffering and sickness by his father until the age of 16. Eventually he married and had a child.

At 29 years old, he decided to leave his life of wealth and privilege, venturing out to find the meaning of all the suffering going on in the world. He continued on his mission for six years, until one day he abandoned his old ways of thinking and instead sat in a mindful meditation underneath a bodhi tree. It was after this moment that Siddhartha Gautama became known the Buddha, or Enlightened one.

Over the next 45 years, the Buddha wandered India, teaching the path he had come to realize in the moment of his Enlightenment. He taught this path to anyone he could, be they rich or poor. As time went on, a community of monks and nuns from all the different caste and tribes began to form around him, devoted to the practice of his teachings. At the age of 80, Buddha passed away. His last words are thought to be "Impermanent are all created things; Strive on with awareness".

After the Buddha's death, his followers continued to orally pass down his teachings and traditions for 200 years before they were written down for future generations. Over the centuries, groups of followers have splintered off and developed their own forms of Buddhism. I'll go over some of the different variations in the later section of this chapter.

Difference Between Buddhism & Other Types of Religion

The main differences found between Buddhism and other types of religion is Buddhism doesn't believe there's a God who controls, creates, and is in charge of the lives of all living things. In Buddhism, happiness and suffering isn't the creation of a God, but is created by every individual being linked together with a karmic force, that's also a part of each individual person.

The Buddha taught his followers that people become who they are not because of their origin or social rank, but because of their personal actions. Buddhism also differs from other religion in that it believes all living beings have the ability to only govern and control themselves, they have no ability to do so for other sentient beings.

Buddhism also teaches that all living beings have their own Buddha inside. That everyone has the ability to become a Buddha. Liberation and Enlightenment are equal truths for everyone, not only a privilege for a select few. This type of equality for all is rarely seen in other religions.

Forms of Buddhism

Buddhism is centered around the belief that our suffering on earth can be relieved if we attain Enlightenment. During the long and storied history of Buddhism, several popular forms have emerged, each of these forms have their own unique spin on the Buddha's teachings, beliefs and practices. In this section, I'll briefly discuss the four dominant forms of Buddhism and what sets them apart from one another. In general, other forms of Buddhism believe in the same teachings of Buddha but put them into practice differently from one another.

Theravada Buddhism

Often lumped together with Hinayana, known as the Small Vehicle. Theravada Buddhism is the oldest form of Buddhism, it's dominant in areas of Southeast Asia, like Cambodia, Thailand, Laos, and Burma. The name Theravada translates to the phrase "Doctrine of Elders". This form of Buddhism is centered around the Pali scriptures, written down from the spoken traditions, or direct teachings from the Buddha himself. By meditating, studying these texts, and also following the Eight Fold Path, these Buddhists believe they'll be able to attain Enlightenment. In this form of Buddhism, a strong emphasis is placed on heeding the advice of those who are wise.

Mahayana Buddhism

Also known as the Great Vehicle. This is the largest form of Buddhism being studied by practitioners today. This form of Buddhism focuses on the concept of compassion, and believes that working out of compassion in order to liberate others from suffering is of the utmost importance. Tibetan Buddhism, Tantric Buddhism, and Pure Land Buddhism all have formed under the banner of Mahayana Buddhism. Some believe Vajrayana to be an offshoot of Mahayana Buddhism while many consider it to be it's own separate branch.

Vajrayana Buddhism

Also known as the Diamond Vehicle or Thunderbolt Vehicle. This form of Buddhism offers a quicker path to finding Enlightenment than any of the other forms I'll be discussing. Followers of this form, believe that the physical has some type of effect upon the spiritual and that the spiritual has a similar effect on the physical. Buddhists following Vajrayana Buddhism encourage chanting, rituals, tantra, and a solid understanding of the other ancient forms of Buddhism. They believe that this is the way to attaining Enlightenment. Vajrayana Buddhism, in the storied history of Buddhism, actually marks a big transition from the speculative thought of Mahayana to the employment of skilled techniques.

Zen Buddhism

This form of Buddhism is credited as being from China, with teachings coming from a monk named Bodhidharma. This form of Buddhism treats daily practice and meditation as the most essential components for finding Enlightenment. This form of Buddhism plays down the role of studying ancient scripture.

Buddhist Concepts

In this section I'm going to discuss two concepts central to Buddhism. These are the Buddhist concepts of Enlightenment and liberation. It's important to have an understanding of each of these concepts, as they play a central role in Buddhism.

Buddhist Concept of Enlightenment

Also referred to as Bodhi, which means full awareness or a full awakening of the Law of Dependent Origination. What is that you might ask? Well, this is physical and mental corporeality on which our lives as human beings are developed. Becoming fully aware, a person is able to overcome any delusions, afflictions, or other impurities. This allows a person to create a life of true happiness and peace. Our capability of awareness is divided up into multiple levels ranging from low to high. This means you can spend your whole life practicing the Dharma, but that doesn't mean you'll ever reach full awareness. Everyone has the ability to become enlightened, but the level of Enlightenment you reach will depend on your karmic force and your mental cohesion of all your past lives.

Buddhist Concept of Liberation

Also referred to as Moksha, which means to liberate, release, or transcend beyond. In Buddhism, liberation consists of different levels ranging from simplicity, all the way to absolute freedom. Whenever a person is able to transcend beyond the afflictions or bondage of hatred, craving, self attachment, ignorance and pride, they reach a new realm of liberation. However, until you're able to liberate yourself from all these afflictions, and no longer be controlled by these mental impurities, you won't be able to experience a true state of liberation.

For a person to reach absolute freedom, a person must eradicate all the roots of their afflictions,as those very impure roots are the the reason for birth and death itself, also known as Samsara. It's important to know that in order to become truly free and liberated, you don't need to travel anywhere else, you can practice right now and right here, in this world, as this person.

Chapter Three: The Four Noble Truths / The Eight Fold Path / The Precepts

In this chapter, you will learn:

- The Four Noble Truths
- The Eight Fold Path
- The Precepts

The Four Noble Truths

These are four truths derived from Buddha's first teaching called "Turning the Wheel of the Dharma." In this teaching, Dharma refers to what truth Buddha had discovered. In this section I'll be going over each of these four truths as they help to comprise the very essence of the Buddha's teachings and are the framework for better understanding Buddhist thought.

The First Noble Truth – The Truth of Suffering.

Often referred to as Dukkha. This truth basically states that all experiences and phenomena are in the end not satisfying. This is because everything is Dukkha, or temporary. Even our life itself is temporary. The Buddha taught us that in before one can understand things like life and death we need to first understand the concept of self.

The Second Noble Truth – The Truth of the Cause of Suffering.

Often referred to as Samudaya. This teaches us that the cause of our suffering is our thirst or cravings. For example, we're always searching for things outside our self in order to attain happiness. However, no matter what success we achieve we never stay satisfied. Buddha teaches us that this thirst for more grows out of our ignorance of self.

People go through their lives reaching for one thing or another in order to be more secure about themselves. Then over time they grow upset when the world around them doesn't behave in a way they think it should.

The ideas of rebirth and karma are often closely associated with this particular Noble Truth.

The Third Noble Truth – The End of Our Suffering.

Often referred to as Nirhodha. This truth holds the hope of us putting an end to our thirst and craving once and for all. Buddha taught that with enough diligence and practice, we can one day put these things aside and reach Enlightenment. Once a person is enlightened this leads to the enlightened person existing in a state of Nirvana.

If the first truth tells us what our illness is, and the second truth gives us what is causing that illness, then the third truth let's us know there's a cure available.

The Fourth Noble Truth – The Path Freeing Us From Suffering.

Often referred to as Magga. Continuing the metaphor above, this truth involves being prescribed a certain treatment by Buddha in order to help cure our suffering.

This treatment is referred to as the Eight Fold Path. In Buddhism one doesn't just believe in ideals and doctrines. Instead, the focus is on living your life around these ideals and doctrines. If followed, one day you may reach Enlightenment and become a Buddha yourself.

The Eight Fold Path

In this section, I'll discuss each step of the Eight Fold Path . The Eight Fold Path is a means by which one can reach Enlightenment. The Buddha explained this path during his first sermon after becoming enlightened. The majority of Buddha's teachings happen to deal with at least some part of this path. It's almost like an outline that helps to pull all his teachings together.

The word samyan or samma is translated as the word right. It means wholesome, wise, ideal, and skillful. It's also used to help describe something that's coherent and complete. When using the word "right" it doesn't mean that you have to do it this way or you're wrong. It's closer to the idea of equilibrium, such as riding the waves in a boat and still being able to remain "right".

The Eight Fold Path is commonly known as the fourth of the Buddhist Four Noble Truths. Those truths are used to help explain our lack of satisfaction with life. The Buddha teaches that only by understanding thoroughly what causes us to be unhappy can we ever resolve it.

The path to reaching this Enlightenment is a difficult one that cannot be achieved quickly or easily. It means we'll need to undergo a major shift in how we relate to, and understand the world all around us. It's through the dedicated practice of the Eight Fold Path that we can one day achieve that understanding.

Practicing the path will reach into every aspect of our lives, every moment of the day. It's not something you can do part time or when you have a spare hour. It's also very important to realize that all of these steps support each other at all times. Therefore, you can't try and master each of these steps one by one. They aren't separate parts, they are one whole.

1. Right Understanding / Right View

This is insight into what the true nature of our reality is. This is a way of seeing that transcends every view. It's a more detached way of viewing things. Practitioners work on this in order to understand how reality actually works. This leads to understanding our suffering, aging, sickness, death, delusion, greed and hatred.

2. Right Intention

This is an unselfish desire of realizing Enlightenment. A practitioner should always be aspiring to get rid of the qualities they know are immoral and wrong. Understanding the right view helps practitioners to understand the differences between wrong intention and right intention.

3. Right Speech

This is the act of using our speech in a compassionate way. Practitioners will abstain from lying and divisive speech. They will also refrain from idle chatter and abusive speech. Practitioners won't say things they know aren't beneficial, untrue or timely.

4. Right Action

This is our ethical conduct. It's our manifestation of compassion. Practitioners try and train themselves to be moral in their activities, and refrain in acting in ways that will bring harm, corrupt themselves, or others. Practitioners should abstain from stealing, taking life, sexual misconduct, and causing harm in any way.

5. Right Livelihood

This the act of making our living through the use of non harmful means. Practitioners are not to work or trade in occupations that will directly, or even indirectly lead to a living being getting harmed.

Some businesses or jobs to steer clear of include, businesses involving weapons or instruments used for harm and business involving harm to human beings. For example, prostitution. It also includes avoiding businesses involving intoxicants or poison, and businesses dealing with meat and the slaughter or breeding of animals.

6. Right Effort

This is the act of cultivating our wholesome qualities, while also releasing all of our unwholesome qualities. Practitioners should try making a persistent effort to rid themselves of all harmful words, deeds and thoughts. Practitioners should instead try to engage in thoughts and actions that would be useful and good to not only themselves, but also others, through their words, deeds, and thoughts.

7. Right Mindfulness

This is the practice of mind and whole body awareness. Practitioners need to always be keeping their minds ready and alert to any phenomena that can affect either the mind or body. They should try and stay deliberate and mindful at all times, making sure that they don't speak or act due to forgetfulness or inattention.

8. Right Concentration

This is the act of our meditation, or of some type of concentrated and dedicated practice. Practitioners need to try and concentrate on one object of attention till they are able to reach a state of full concentration and meditative absorption. This practice can be developed by using mindful breathing, repetition of phrases, or visualization.

The Eight Fold Path can be divided up into three different sections. These are ethical conduct, wisdom, and mental discipline.

The Path of Wisdom

Right Intention and Right view make up this path. Right Intention is the commitment and energy a person needs in order to be engaged fully in the practice of Buddhism. The Right View isn't based on beliefs and doctrines but in our perception of the true nature of the world we live in and ourselves.

The Path of Ethical Conduct

Right Livelihood, Right Action, and Right Speech make up this path. This path calls out to us to be compassionate in how we speak, and our actions to others. It also means doing no harm to anyone else in our daily lives, while cultivating personal wholesomeness. This part of the Eight Fold Path ties into the Five Precepts which I'll be discussing in the next section.

The Path of Mental Discipline

Right Concentration, Right Mindfulness, and Right Effort make up this path. It's imperative we fully develop our mental discipline in order to cut through any delusions. Most forms of Buddhism actually encourage its practitioners to meditate in order to focus their minds and achieve clarity.

The Precepts

In this section I'm going to discuss what are known as the Precepts of Buddhism. Usually religions have ethical and moral rules that act as commandments. Buddhism has a set of Precepts. I must stress, it's important to know that these aren't a list of rules that need to be followed.

In most religions many of the laws are believed to originate from God, so breaking any of those laws can be seen as transgression or sin against God. Buddhism on the other hand doesn't have a God, so breaking the Precepts while not looked well upon, are also not transgressions or sins against God.

There are different sets of Precepts you'll run across in Buddhism. Depending on what school of thought you follow these may differ from one another. You'll commonly find that there are five, ten, and even sixteen different Precepts. Some orders even have lists that are longer than that.

The Five Precepts

The most common list is known as the Five Precepts. For many Buddhists, these are considered the basic ones that should be followed.

1. Abstain from killing.

2. Abstain from lying.

3. Abstain from stealing.

4. Abstain from sexual misconduct.

5. Abstain from abusing any intoxicants.

It's important to know that by following the Precepts, you're training yourself to behave like a Buddha would.

The Ten Grand Precepts

This list of Precepts expands upon the Five Precepts with an additional set of precepts.

1. Abstain from killing.

2. Abstain from lying.

3. Abstain from stealing.

4. Abstain from sexual misconduct.

5. Abstain from abusing any intoxicants.

6. Abstain from blaming others and elevating oneself.

7. Abstain from talking about other people's faults and errors.

8. Abstain from being stingy.

9. Abstain from being angry.

10. Abstain from speaking any ill of any of the Three Treasures.

The Three Pure Precepts

Many Mahayana Buddhists also vow to always uphold what are known as the Three Pure Precepts.

1. To always do good

2. To never do no evil

3. To save all living beings

The word "kusula" and the word "aksula" are often translated to the "good" and "evil" mentioned in the above precepts, but they can also be translated as "skillful" and as "unskillful". Basically a "skillful" action brings a person closer to becoming enlightened and an "unskillful" action leads a person further away from becoming enlightened.

The last precept about saving all living beings is a vow promising to bring all living being to eventual Enlightenment.

The Sixteen Bodhisattva Precepts

These refer to the Ten Grand Precepts and also the Three Pure Precepts along with what are referred to as the Three Refuges.

1. I take my refuge in Buddha.

2. I take my refuge in Dharma.

3. I take my refuge in Sangha.

Chapter Four: Karma, Rebirth & Reincarnation

In this chapter, you will learn:

- Karma & Buddhism
- Rebirth, Reincarnation & Buddhism

Karma & Buddhism

In terms of Buddhism, karma is normally defined as a willful action that is driven by our intention and leads to future consequences. Many people think that this term means something to do with fate or a sense of cosmic justice. They think karma is the result of someone's actions.

That's not what Buddhists view the term to mean. Buddhists believe that karma is the action itself not the results of the action. Buddhists believe the law of karma is simply a law of cause and effect.

For Buddhists, the concept of karma is complex and non-linear. Buddhism views the present as being shaped by both our present and past actions. What we do in the moment shapes things now and later down the road. This means that we don't need to feel resigned and powerless already bound by fate.

Every moment has new potential because what we do is what happens to us. Change is always a possibility. To change our lives and to change our karma we simply need to change our minds and any repetitive patterns we've fallen into over time.

Buddhism also teaches us that outside forces besides our karma will shape and impact our lives. Some things that will do so can include natural forces like gravity, sudden natural disasters, and even the changing of seasons. When something bad does occur it's isn't a form of punishment. Rather, it's an event that's unfortunate and requires not judgment but compassion.

Remember Buddhism does not teach or believe there to be some mysterious force or God who doles out rewards and punishment for people it deems good or bad. Karma is not a form of moral justice. Karma does not reward or punish. It's not the result, instead it's the action you take. Karma is a natural law and doesn't have anything to do with rewarding or punishing people.

Rebirth, Reincarnation & Buddhism

Most cultures view reincarnation as a form transmigration of our souls to a different body after we have died. In Buddhism, there's no teaching for this. In fact, one of the most basic doctrines in Buddhism is that of "anatta". What is that? Well, it means no self or no soul. Basically, it means there is no type of permanent spirit or essence of our individual self able to survive our death.

Buddha often taught that we view as our permanent self, is nothing more than an illusion that is created by "skandhas" or the five aggregates. These are how our bodies, emotional sensations, consciousness, beliefs, and ideas work together to deceive us into believing there is a distinctive permanent self.

The Five Skandhas

These are the five physical and psychological aggregates, that according to the Buddha, are the very basis of our constant self grasping. These are in essence. blockages preventing us from reaching Enlightenment. They come in all forms, from mental and physical, to material and spiritual. The Buddha's teachings taught us that the individual is merely a combination of all five aggregates or skandhas of existence.

In Buddhism, the idea is to examine what is known as the "self" more accurately. We can do this by making use of, and exploring these five aggregates or skandhas. By better knowing ourselves, the hope is we can one day move past all our defilement and disillusions. Remember, the skandhas aren't you. They are only conditioned phenomena that is temporary. Once you realize these aren't you, you'll be on the path to Enlightenment.

1. Form

Some forms include elements like water, earth, wind, and fire. There are also the things that are made from each of these elements. You can include the five senses in this section as well.

2. Perception

This can be either conceptual or non-conceptual. It's the knowledge that puts things together. For example, when we see a shirt we know it's a shirt because we are able to associate it with our prior experiences with shirts.

The non-conceptual perceptions include our five senses and the conceptual perceptions include things like ideas and thoughts.

In each case, perception can be either discerning or it can be non-discerning.

For instance our non-conceptual five senses are considered to be discerning when operating normally, perceiving there proper objects, such as shapes, smells, sounds, tastes, and textures. Mental perception is discerning when distinguishing things like names and identities.

Perceptions are considered to be experienced subjectively. Buddhist teachings say our perceptions are important because they make the basis for our disagreements.

3. Feeling

This references sensations not our emotional feelings. These sensations are thought of as pleasant, painful or neutral. They are both sensations of the mind and of the body.

Buddhist teachings value feelings as important because they form the basis of both aversion and attachment. These two things are the root of most conflicts between people who have not been Enlightened.

4. Consciousness

This refers to our consciousness of the impressions we get from our fives senses, including from mental objects, like our ideas, thoughts and emotions.

Consciousness is our sensitivity or awareness to any object without conceptualizing it. It's considered by many to be our base, helping to tie all of our experiences in life together.

5. Formations

These refer to our thoughts and our emotions. It refers to our mental states. Some teachings refer to 51 important states. I won't be going over all of them here but to give you an idea, a few of these include diligence, absence of attachment, conscientiousness, faith, absence of delusion, absence of aggression, ignorance, anger, doubt, desire, harmful belief, and pride

The Three Marks of Existence

Buddhism teaches that everything in our physical world, which includes psychological experiences and mental activity, is marked by three distinct characteristics. These are suffering, impermanence, and a lack of ego. It's through our awareness and examination of these three marks that we can liberate ourselves from the clinging and grasping that are binding us to delusion and illusion.

1. Impermanence or Anicca

This is a core property of everything conditioned. All things are constantly in a state of flux and are therefore impermanent. Since everything is in flux it means that liberation is always a possibility.

2. Suffering or Dukkha

Also means imperfect or unsatisfactory. All things mental and material that have not been liberated are Dukkha. This means that even pleasant experiences and things that are beautiful are Dukkha. Hence the term "life is suffering".

3. Lack of Ego or Anatta

Also known as non-self. This teaching means that you aren't an autonomous, integral entity. The individual ego or self is simply a byproduct of skandhas. It's important to understand that skandhas are empty. These aren't qualities individuals can posses, since there is no actual self to possess them.

Buddhism believes that not only is nothing carried from life to life but nothing is even carried over from moment to moment. Instead, everything including all living beings, are constantly in a state of flux. Everything is always changing, everything is always becoming, and everything is always dying.

People like to turn to doctrines and religion in order to get simplified answers for unknowable questions. Buddhism isn't set up that way. Just believing in something whether it's rebirth or reincarnation serves no actual purpose. Buddhism practices seeing illusion for the illusion it is and seeing reality as   reality.

The Buddha's teachings show us that our often delusional belief in a sense of self causes most of our dissatisfaction in life. Once we are able to experience illusion for the illusion it really is we can finally become liberated.

Chapter Five: The Seven Factors of Enlightenment & The Five Hindrances

In this chapter, you will learn:

- The Seven Factors of Enlightenment
- The Five Hindrances
- The Four Absorptions
- Renunciation

The Seven Factors of Enlightenment

In this section I'm going to discuss the Seven Factors of Enlightenment and what they involve. These are seven qualities that both describe and lead to eventual Enlightenment. These factors are also seen as great antidotes for the Five Hindrances which I will be discussing further in the next section.

1. Mindfulness

This is also a part of the Eight Fold Path, and is crucial to the proper practice of Buddhism. Mindfulness is mind and whole body awareness during the present moment. When you're mindful, you're fully present, not off daydreaming or worrying about other things.

Being mindful also means that you must release any habits of the mind that help to maintain your illusion of having a separate individual self. Being mindful doesn't judge between disliking or liking. Being mindful means you're dropping all your conceptualizations. For example when mindful breathing, your focus is just on breath not on "your" breath.

2. Investigation

This is a deep look into the very nature of our reality. It's an analytic approach in many ways. It is an investigation of both Buddha's doctrines and the nature of what we call existence. Buddha always taught his followers to never blindly accept something on faith alone. Instead, they should thoroughly investigate what he taught, so they could come to terms with the truth for themselves.

3. Energy

This factor plays an important role, as the quest for one's Enlightenment requires unending courage and strength. One needs energy in order to achieve. One also needs to always advance and not falter. Only through dogged determination and diligence can one hope to attain Enlightenment.

4. Happiness

A famous quote by the 14th Dalai Lama says that ""Happiness is not something ready made. It comes from your own actions." This means that it's the things we do, not the things we get, that grows our happiness.

Buddhism teaches us that craving things that we believe are outside of ourselves only further binds us to our suffering. Once we understand this, we can start to let go of these cravings and find true happiness.

5. Tranquility

This factor deals with tranquility or calmness of our consciousness and body. While the last factor was more about a joyful type of happiness, this factor is focused more on the contentment felt, of someone who's finished their work and is at rest.

Like the previous factor this factor cannot be contrived or forced. It will happen naturally as we attain the other factors.

6. Concentration

Another part of the Eight Fold Path. This factor differs from being mindful in that concentration requires we focus all our mental faculties onto a single mental or physical object, while practicing the Four Absorptions. I'll discuss what those are in a later section of this chapter.

Concentration is in essence, a slowing down of our consciousness and mental activity by focusing on single point. When mastered, all sense of our individual self will disappear and both the object and the subject are absorbed completely into one another.

7. Equanimity

In Buddhism, this refers to the balance between the extremes of desire and aversion. Basically, it's not allowing yourself to be swayed in either direction by the things you like or dislike. It's an evenness of our mind. It's a sense of freedom that can't be upset from loss or gain, blame or praise, pain or pleasure. Achieving equanimity allows us to be indifferent to the demands of our ego, and all it's cravings. It doesn't affect our mindset toward the well being of others around us. When it comes to others we are not indifferent.

The Five Hindrances

The Buddha's teachings taught us that five hindrances exist that stop us from reaching Enlightenment. These mental states are known as hindrances because they help bind us to our suffering and ignorance. Realizing our Enlightenment means freeing ourselves of these hindrances.

Hindrances can't be ignored or pushed under the rug. They will only go away once we've realized they are states we've created for ourselves. Once we are able to perceive this, we can begin the path towards Enlightenment.

For hindrances, one must practice and meditate. The initial step is recognizing the hindrance, then acknowledging it, and finally understanding you're the one who's making it real.

1. Sensual Desire

This refers to anything from the desire for sex to desiring certain foods. When these feelings arise the first thing to do is recognize your feeling, acknowledge it and then try and just observe the desire and not give in to it or chase the feeling.

2. Ill Will

Feeling anger and rage is often an easy to spot hindrance. The cure for this is to try and cultivate metta or loving kindness. Metta is a virtue that Buddha taught should be used in times of ill will and anger.

We often get angry because someone has bruised our ego. One needs to practice letting go of anger, acknowledging its presence, while also acknowledging that anger is born from our own pride and ignorance.

3. Sloth, Drowsiness. or Torpor

Many people find they have trouble keeping up there energy or staying awake during meditation. The Buddha taught that we should always pay attention to the thoughts we are chasing when getting tired, and then shift the mind somewhere else. If that doesn't work, try switching to a walking meditation, pinching yourself, or splashing water on your face.

If this type of drowsiness occurs on a regular basis, as you constantly feel low on energy, you need to find out if there's some type of psychological or physical cause. Any health issues should always be resolved in a timely fashion.

4. Worry and Restlessness

This particular hindrance comes in many different forms. Some of these forms include remorse, anxiety, and feeling rushed. Trying to meditate when in this state of mind is not a comfortable proposition.

If you're in an anxious state of mind don't try and force the anxiety away. Instead try to imagine your body as if it were a container. Observe the anxiousness moving around freely, don't attempt to separate or control it.

People suffering PSTD or chronic anxiety disorders may find meditating to be incredibly intense. It some cases you many need to find psychological assistance before trying to start practicing any intensive meditating.

5. Skepticism or Uncertainty

Doubt and skepticism aren't good or bad. In reality, it's something you can start working with. Never ignore doubt or tell yourself to avoid feeling doubt. Instead, keep yourself open to what your skepticism and doubt are trying to warn you about.

Throughout life we often get discouraged when our experience practicing meditation doesn't quite live up to what we expected. This is why it's important to remain unattached to any expectation. The effectiveness of our meditation sessions will differ over time. Some meditation sessions could get deep, while other could be filled with frustration.

Don't let those tough periods get you down. Oftentimes, in the end they bear the most beautiful of fruit. That's why it's important not to label our meditation sessions as being good or bad. Avoid attaching any expectations.

The Four Absorptions

Absorption is often referred to as Jhana. These Jhana are stages of development in the Right Concentration, which is part of the Eight Fold Path. Jhana refers to our mind being entirely absorbed in concentration. Jhana also relates to the word Jhapeti, meaning "burn up." Jhana is seen as burning away of our confusion and defilement.

The Buddha's teachings discussed four levels of Jhana. However, over time eight levels came into fruition. These eight levels can be split into two sections. The first is Rupajhana or the lower level. The second is Arupajhana or the higher level. The lower levels are referred to as form meditations and the higher levels are often referred to as formless meditations.

Some Buddhist schools of thought use the Jhanas to measure the progress of students. Others believe that these measurements can lead to attachments being formed and are an obstacle on the road to Enlightenment.

The Rupajhanas

The first Jhana will be marked by happiness and rapture.

The second Jhana will find the analytic mind stilled as the practitioner enters a state of pure awareness that is free from any type of conceptualizations. A feeling of rapture will also permeate the body.

The third Jhana will find the sense of rapture subsiding only to be replaced with a sense of full body pleasure. The practitioner is also more alert and mindful.

Finally, the fourth Jhana will find the practitioner infused with bright and pure awareness as all their sensations of pain and pleasure melt away.

The Arupajhanas

These Jhanas are often referred to as a peaceful immaterial liberation that transcends all material form. These Jhanas are usually known for their boundless space, objective spheres, nothingness, and boundless consciousness.

These objects will become more subtle, when each one is mastered the preceding object will fall away. Eventually only a subtle perception will remain.

Renunciation

This is a word that comes up often when discussing Buddhism. I wanted to devote a section to going over what it means to those who practice.

In English, the word "renounce" means to relinquish or give away. It also means to disown or reject. Some may view this as penance or a form of punishment but renunciation in Buddhism is different.

For Buddhists this word is most often related back to a term that means "to go forth". It's usually used when describing the act of a nun or monk going into a life of homelessness to be liberated from their lust.

In a broad sense, renunciation can be viewed as letting go of the things that bind us to our suffering and ignorance. Buddha taught us that true renunciation means we need to thoroughly perceive how we've made ourselves unhappy through greediness and grasping for more. Therefore, when we do finally follow through on our renunciation, it's a liberating and positive act, not some form of punishment.

Remember, enjoyment of something itself isn't a bad thing or cause for renunciation. If you eat something you enjoy, you don't need to throw it out. Your goal is to enjoy the food without any attachment to it. Only eat what you need for substance without overeating and being greedy. The same principle applies to most other things and our possessions as well.

Chapter Six: Buddhism Rituals and Meditation

In this chapter, you will learn:

- Buddhism Rituals
- Buddhism Meditation

Buddhism Rituals

When practitioners are practicing at home or coming to a temple to honor Buddha, many will perform rituals in the process. Some of the common rituals include chanting, bowing, praying, eating a vegetarian meal, meditating, and celebrating Buddhist holidays like Buddha's day of birth. In this section, I'll discuss a few of these rituals briefly.

Bowing

Bowing is also referred to as prostration. When a practitioner enters into a room where a Buddha statue rests, they will put both their palms together while bowing to show respect for Buddha and all he has taught us. The practitioner will bow three times facing the statue and kneeling with palms both turned upward while on a stool for kneeling.

Opening one's palms is representative of compassion and wisdom during the first bow or prostration. Then, you turn out a single hand to symbolize the cultivation of internal wisdom, while moving your other hand. This means the offering outwards of compassion.

The second bow or prostration indicates Buddha's bestowal of compassion and wisdom upon the practitioner. The third bow or prostration shows the practitioners sincerity of prayer to Buddha. In all, it takes three bows or prostrations in order to emphasize earnestness and build up the proper concentration.

Chanting

A Buddhist chant is speech that's pure. It's free of curses, lies, slander, and negativity. Chanting is uttering the teachings of Buddha, thereby training our thoughts through constant repetition to be a vision of perseverance, benevolence, charity, and self discipline.

Gongs are often used as a chanting instruments during Buddhist ceremonies. Gongs are used primarily for three different purposes. First, to announce a meeting time. Second, to mark different service phases or chanting tempos. Third, to help aid the practitioners during the course of meditation.

Lighting Incense

Burning or lighting incense is a gesture used to pay the highest respects to Buddha. A piece of incense being lit, prompts us to better follow the practices and teachings of Buddha, while training our mind to only focus on a singular object while meditating.

The act of actually lighting the incense, helps remind us to free ourselves from life's constant cycle of life and death from reincarnation, mental affliction, and attachment to our more material desires. Practicing with incense can help to guide us during our journey through spiritual development.

Altar Offerings

You'll often find in temples, tables laid out with flowers and fresh fruits placed on them. Buddhists will then place items on these altars to show appreciation for Buddha and his teachings. This is most commonly seen on Chinese New Years, as thousands of practitioners will go to temple with their offerings to thank Buddha for a harmonious and safe year.

Offerings at temples are normally fresh flowers and fruit. Occasionally you'll also see smaller vegetarian dishes. In essence all the offerings of food are vegetarian, since Buddhism advocates being vegetarian to avoid killing or harm animals for food.

Buddhism Meditation

Meditating is about our mind and purifying it. It's a technique used to develop the concentration that can only be gotten through having direct experiences, not only from reading. The purpose behind meditation is calming our wandering minds. Buddhist meditation includes a variety of different meditation techniques, squarely aimed at tranquility, concentration, and insight.

The first step to calm the mind is Samadhi. One must focus on a single object while directing our false minds so it will no longer engage in any type of egotistical thought. This step is followed by self contemplation or Vipassana. This is the process where we get our minds under control, while engaging in introspective contemplation.

Meditation is the adjustment of our breath, mind, and body. First let's discuss body adjustment. This is where you sit upright, keeping your legs crossed with your hands placed on knees. Next, close both eyes, while keeping your head up and back straight. If for some reason you can't keep your legs crossed, you can sit using a chair.

The second adjustment is the breath adjustment. Breathing is a crucial part of meditation. Be sure to concentrate on where air will enter into your nostrils.

The final adjustment is the mind adjustment. Be very conscious of your breath as you're inhaling and exhaling. Whenever air goes in your nose, count to one in your mind. Don't count when air is exiting the nose. Count to ten using this method, before repeating again from one.

If you meditate regularly, thought will eventually weaken, concentration will strengthen and you'll find moments of inner peace and deep calm. When starting out it's good to meditate for approximately 15-20 minutes each day, extending your time 5 minutes every week until you've gotten to a point of meditating 45 minutes a day.

There are several variations and types of meditation you can engage in. These include Vipassana meditation, Loving-kindness meditation, Zen meditation, and Mindfulness meditation just to name a few. Each one will slightly differ from the other. I suggest checking out my resource section for places you can find more in detail explanations of each form of meditation, their intentions, and how to properly practice them in your daily life.

Chapter Seven: Buddhism & Daily Life

In this chapter, you will learn:

- Buddhism & Daily Life

Buddhism & Daily Life

Most people think that living a spiritual life on a daily basis means we need to ignore or somehow neglect our daily lives. This is far from true. Becoming a spiritual person means becoming the realest version of yourself. Being a kind person is the greatest thing we can do in our lives.

So how do we go about cultivating a kind and loving heart on a daily basis. It's not   enough for us to tell ourselves how to feel and how to act. When you fill yourself with ideas of things you should do, you'll often only end up feeling guilty for not becoming what you think you should be. In order to make a real change you need to transform your mind. You need to learn how to become less self centered, and you need to want to honestly become a kindhearted person.

Each morning, after waking up, before leaving our bed and thinking about breakfast or work, you need to start your day off thinking about a mantra you find puts you in a good state of mind. I like to start off my day by repeating this mantra:

"Today I'll do as little harm as I can. Today I'm going to try and benefit others whenever possible. Today I only want to take part in actions that will help others attain happiness."

Starting off the day with positive intention is extremely beneficial. I find that when I'm setting my motivations the moment I wake up, I don't allow negativity to worm it's way into my mind and pull me out of my positive mindset.

After getting ready for the day and before heading off to work I suggest, meditating or reciting your prayers. This puts you in a great head space to have a successful day.

Now if you don't have enough time to meditate in the morning, make sure to make time at some point in the day. Daily meditation is crucial. I know life is busy and it can be hard to make time, but you need to make your path to Enlightenment a priority in your life. When you respect yourself in a spiritual manner, you'll find you'll respect yourself more, and respect others who are around you.

While I prefer carving out some time for morning meditation, I know this can be difficult for some people, especially those with kids. If you can't wake up an hour before everyone else in your household, you can try having your kids or spouse meditate with you. If you don't have time for some other reason besides family, try and make time during the afternoon, if you're at home, or early evening when you get home from work.

After you've left the house and headed to work, how do you go about practicing Dharma in the workplace? Well, remember your mantra and make an effort to be kind to everyone around you. Some people also uses frequent events that happen during the day as triggers, in order to help bring them back to a proper state of mind. These things can be anything from the phone ringing, to being stopped at a red light. Once a trigger occurs, train yourself to stop for a moment and go over your mantra. Eventually when these triggers occur in the future you're mind will conditioned to think of your mantra automatically.

During the day try and be as mindful as possible. Be aware of your feelings, what you're saying, and what you're thinking. Don't just coast through the day spaced out on autopilot. Be present and experience your life instead of only reacting to it. For example, I used to always be guilty of going on autopilot when driving, I can remember making wrong turns because I was on automatic pilot. I wasn't focusing on the moment. Now I practice mindfulness all the time, no matter the situation.

Cultivating mindfulness is a key component to Buddhism and should be an area of focus in your daily life. Combined with meditation it makes for a powerful one two punch. Once you become more mindful of yourself and your actions, you can start becoming more mindful of others and the world around you. This will only benefit you in the long run.

Every evening before bed, I like to study and do a review of my entire day. I take some time to go through my day and see what areas I can improve on the following day. I like to reflect on everything that occurred and really mull it over. When I find things I'm unhappy about, I like to remedy them. I do this by performing a purification service, forgiving myself, and letting go of the negative energy I was feeling. This allows me to clean myself up emotionally and begin the next day anew. I also find it aids in my sleep and overall feeling of restfulness during the night. I no longer have the weight of negative energy on my mind.

As you can see from this small breakdown, practicing Buddhism in your daily life doesn't need to be something that consumes you. Just direct your mind with positive intention, carve out some time for meditation, practice mindfulness, and review each day before bed. You can also do additional things like read scripture or practice rituals but I leave that up to you. Everyone has their own specific routine they prefer to follow. Just remember, by transforming your attitude even when in the middle of your normal daily activities, your life will become much more meaningful.

Chapter Eight: Buddhist Tips, Quotes & Resources

In this chapter, you will learn:

- 10 Quick Buddhist Tips & Tricks For A Happier Life
- A Brief Guide to Buddhist Apps & Resources
- 21 Buddhist Quotes to Motivate

10 Quick Buddhist Tips & Tricks For A Happier Life

In this section I'm going to share some 10 quick tips and tricks anyone following the path of Buddhism should know. Hopefully you'll find them to be useful.

1. Smile more. It might feel forced at first, but over time you'll find it comes much more naturally and plays a big part in changing your overall mood. I also found it to be quite the stress reliever. Remember, it takes less muscles to smile than it does to frown.

2. If you're having problems meditating try yoga. Yoga is a great way to take your focus away from your thoughts and place it on breath. Yoga can also be relaxing, which helps to ease the mind. Yoga allows you to keep present in the moment. These are all things that will come in handy when meditating.

3. Stay surrounded with positive people. The less you're around negativity and negative people, the less chance you'll have spiraling into negativity yourself. Negative thinking needs fuel to survive, don't feed the beast.

4. Change up the intention of what you're thinking from something negative to something positive. For example, instead of thinking this car ride is going to take forever, think this time will give me more time to practice mindfulness and enjoy the company of the people I'm driving with. Do this enough and your mindset will shift to thinking this way naturally.

5. You responsible for your life. Don't play the victim card. Instead be the hero of your story. You always have choices. Nothing is permanent. Things can always change if you make them.

6. Help the people around you. Whether it's friends, family, or strangers always be willing to go the extra mile for someone else and lend a helping hand. Not only is it the kind thing to do, it also feels better to give.

7. Nobody's perfect. People will make mistakes. Let yourself forgive and move forward. It can be easy to harp on past mistakes. Don't waste the time and energy. It serves no purpose.

8. Make a list of things you're grateful for. I like to do this weekly. I find it helps to center me and keep my mind focused on the important things in my life. I like to jot down at least 5 to 10 things I'm grateful about in my life.

9. Read some positive and inspiring quotes. I've included some you can start with in a later section of this chapter. I've found quotes to be big motivators. I keep some handy that I can read whenever I'm feeling low or uninspired.

10. Sing A Song. Singing helps express our feeling and relieve stress. I've always found it to have an immediate and positive effect on my mood. You don't need to remember all the lyrics or have a great voice. Just sing a song and see how you feel afterwards.

A Brief Guide to Buddhist Apps & Resources

Here are a ton of great resources I've found that will help you along in your studies. I've listed some apps and websites with plenty of reference material to help you out with any of your questions. I've also included a small list of books I've found to be both inspiring and beneficial.

Apps to Download

Buddhify

Available on both IOS and Android. This app is a great tool for practicing mindfulness with over 80 mindfulness meditations included, along with ways to track and monitor your progress. This is a paid app. Costs $2.99 on Android and $4.99 on IOS

Buddha Mind

Available on IOS only. When wearing a compatible Bluetooth heart rate monitor this app allows you to measure and track your heart rate during meditations and other activities. Now you can see what type of results meditation is having on your body over time. This is a paid app. Costs $2.99.

Equanimity

Available on IOS only. Another app dedicated to meditations. Offers timers and trackers to see your progress over time. Also has a great feature where you can enter any thoughts and feelings you had during each meditation session. This is a paid app. Costs $4.99.

The Ultimate Buddhism Library

Available on IOS only. This is a collection of 50 books pertaining to Buddhism all in one spot. Get a complete grasp of Buddhism right on your phone. These books cover Southern Buddhism, Northern Buddhism, Modern Works and Jataka. This is a paid app. Costs $0.99

Daily Buddhist Prayers

Available on IOS and Android. Have your daily prayers all in one place. Listen to Buddhist prayers recited by real monks. This is a paid app. Costs $0.99 droid and $1.99 on IOS.

Insight Timer

Available on IOS and Android. This app is a meditation timer which also functions as a guide to mindfulness. People using the app can share all their meditation times with other users and friends. They can also check in on different people meditating in their area. This app also comes with guided meditations from teachers like Jack Kornfield, Sharon Salzberg and Elisha Goldstein. Finally this app also comes with a timer that will allow you to keep time of your meditation. This app is free to download but does have in app purchases of $4.99.

Buddha's Brain

Available on IOS only. Great app with strong strategies for rewiring your brain. Also offers guided meditations. This is a paid app. Costs $4.99

Resources to Visit

Buddhist eLibrary

This is an amazing resource that is completely free. Files can be downloaded in the forms of PDF files on just about anything related to Buddhism. Also comes with audio, video, and image libraries. Not the easiest as far as getting around due to having to download material and then sift through it. However, the sheer volume of free information more than makes up for it.

Buddhanet's World Buddhist Directory

Great free resource that is also available as a free app on both IOS and Android. This site allows you to find Buddhist related organizations and meditation groups wherever you are in the world,

Buddhist TV Channel

Online site dedicated to Buddhist issues and news throughout the world. Also has tons of articles and resources for all things Buddhism, including opinion articles, podcasts, and other important issues.

Books to Check Out

What the Buddha Taught by Walpola Rahula

The Art of Living: Vipassana Meditation as Taught By S.N. Goenka by William Hart

In the Buddha's Words: An Anthology of Discourses from the Pali Canon by Bhikkhu Bodhi

Peace Is Every Step: The Path of Mindfulness in Everyday Life by Thich Nhat Hanh

The Wisdom of No Escape and the Path of Loving-Kindness by Pema Chodron

The Heart of the Buddha's Teaching: Transforming Suffering into Peace, Joy, and Liberation by Thich Nhat Hanh

Start Where You Are: A Guide to Compassionate Living by Pema Chodron

Real Happiness: The Power of Meditation: A 28-Day Program by Sharon Salzberg

21 Buddhist Quotes to Motivate

In this section I'm going to share some quotes pertaining to Buddhism that I found to be inspiring, powerful, or motivational. Hopefully they'll make you think or bring a smile to your face.

1. "Greater in battle than the man who would conquer a thousand-thousand men, is he who would conquer just one — himself. Better to conquer yourself than others. When you've trained yourself, living in constant self-control, neither a deva nor gandhabba, nor a Mara banded with Brahmas, could turn that triumph back into defeat." — Gautama Buddha

2. "It is impossible to build one's own happiness on the unhappiness of others. This perspective is at the heart of Buddhist teachings." — Daisaku Ikeda

3. "Purity or impurity depends on oneself, No one can purify another." — Gautama Buddha

4. "We need the courage to learn from our past and not live in it." — Sharon Salzberg

5. "The secret of Buddhism is to remove all ideas, all concepts, in order for the truth to have a chance to penetrate, to reveal itself." — Thích Nhất Hạnh,

6. "People get into a heavy-duty sin and guilt trip, feeling that if things are going wrong, that means that they did something bad and they are being punished. That's not the idea at all. The idea of karma is that you continually get the teachings that you need to open your heart. To the degree that you didn't understand in the past how to stop protecting your soft spot, how to stop armoring your heart, you're given this gift of teachings in the form of your life, to give you everything you need to open further." — Pema Chödrön

7. "Long is the night to him who is awake; long is a mile to him who is tired; long is life to the foolish who do not know the true law." — Gautama Buddha

8. "When you dig a well, there's no sign of water until you reach it, only rocks and dirt to move out of the way. You have removed enough; soon the pure water will flow," said Buddha." — Deepak Chopra

9. "Searching outside of you is Samsara (the world). Searching within you leads to Nirvana." — Amit Ray

10. "How wonderful it would be if people did all they could for one other without seeking anything in return! One should never remember a kindness done, and never forget a kindness received." — Kentetsu Takamori

11. "True change is within; leave the outside as it is." — Dalai Lama XIV

12. "Whatever a monk keeps pursuing with his thinking and pondering, that becomes the inclination of his awareness." — Gautama Buddha

13. "Service which is rendered without joy helps neither the servant nor the served. But all other pleasures and possessions pale into nothingness before service which is rendered in a spirit of joy." — Mahatma Gandhi

14. "Mindfulness helps us get better at seeing the difference between what's happening and the stories we tell ourselves about what's happening, stories that get in the way of direct experience. Often such stories treat a fleeting state of mind as if it were our entire and permanent self." — Sharon Salzberg

15. "The Way is not in the sky; the Way is in the heart." — Gautama Buddha

16. "Being vegetarian here also means that we do not consume dairy and egg products, because they are products of the meat industry. If we stop consuming, they will stop producing. Only collective awakening can create enough determination for action." — Thích Nhất Hạnh

17. "If you want to take care of tomorrow, take better care of today. We always live now. All we have to do is entrust ourselves to the life we now live." — Dainin Katagiri

18. "We don't need any sort of religious orientation to lead a life that is ethical, compassionate & kind." — Sharon Salzberg

19. "If there is any religion that could respond to the needs of modern science, it would be Buddhism." — Albert Einstein

20. "We are not going in circles, we are going upwards. The path is a spiral; we have already climbed many steps." — Hermann Hesse

21. "You only lose what you cling to." — Gautama Buddha

Conclusion

Thanks again for purchasing this book on Buddhism. I hope that you've found the information provided to be helpful and informative. Buddhism is purely based on our own experiences, morality, practice, rationalism and insights. Buddhism doesn't force blind allegiance to a set of Gods or dogmas. The core of Buddhism is not as much about faith but about bettering yourself though diligence, mindfulness, meditation and self reflection.

Many people view Buddhism as more philosophy than traditional religion. However you view it, Buddhism and its teachings are a guide to an incredibly effective way of transforming your life and securing long lasting happiness. The experiences shared from thousands of years of Buddhist traditions has created an amazing resource for anyone who wants to follow the path to a happier life culminating in Enlightenment.

Remember nothing is permanent, you're actions will definitely have consequences, and change is always possible. If the teachings of Buddhism speak to you, I suggest checking out the resource section and begin the process. It's never too late to make a change in your life.

I hope you find the path you're looking for after reading this book.

Good luck! I wish you nothing but the best!

Made in the USA
Middletown, DE
29 November 2018